My Amazing Body

EATING

Angela Royston

www.raintreepublishers.co.uk
Visit our website to find out more information about **Raintree** books.

To order:
☎ Phone 44 (0) 1865 888112
🖹 Send a fax to 44 (0) 1865 314091
💻 Visit the Raintree bookshop at **www.raintreepublishers.co.uk** to browse our catalogue and order online.

First published in Great Britain by Raintree,
Halley Court, Jordan Hill, Oxford OX2 8EJ,
part of Harcourt Education.
Raintree is a registered trademark of Harcourt
Education Ltd.

© Harcourt Education Ltd 2004
The moral right of the proprietor has been asserted.

Editorial: Nick Hunter and Catherine Clarke
Design: Kim Saar and Roslyn Broder
Illustrations: Ken Vail Graphic Design p. 5 and
Will Hobbs p. 29
Picture Research: Maria Joannou and Pete Morris
Production: Jonathan Smith

Originated by Dot Gradations Ltd
Printed and bound in China by South China
Printing Company

ISBN 1 844 43384 6
08 07 06 05 04
10 9 8 7 6 5 4 3 2 1

British Library Cataloguing in Publication Data
Royston, Angela.
Eating. - (My Amazing Body)
612.3
A full catalogue record for this book is available from the British Library.

Acknowledgements
The publishers would like to thank the following for permission to reproduce photographs:
Corbis pp. **6**, **8**, **15**, **17** (Michael and Patricia Fogden); FLPA pp. **7** (Minden Pictures), **9** (Jurgen and Christine Sohns), **13** (Gerar Lacz); Gareth Boden p. **10**; Getty Images (Imagebank) p. **4**; Nicolas Beresford-Davies p. **26**; Pete Morris pp. **12**, **14**, **27**, **28**; Science Photo Library pp. **11** (Prof. P. Motta/Department of Anatomy, University "La Sapienza", Rome), **16**, **18**, **19**, **20**, **21** (Eye of Science), **22**, **23** (CNRI), **24** (Hattie Young), **25** (Dr Linda Stannard, UCT).

Cover photograph of a coloured X-ray of human intestines, reproduced with permission of Science Photo Library (CNRI) and of a child eating, reproduced with permission of Photodisc.

The publishers would like to thank Carol Ballard for her assistance in the preparation of this book.

Every effort has been made to contact copyright holders of any material reproduced in this book. Any omissions will be rectified in subsequent printings if notice is given to the publishers.

The paper used to print this book comes from sustainable resources.

Contents

Any words appearing in bold, **like this**, are explained in the Glossary.

Inside and out

All living things have to eat food and drink water to survive. Most people rely on farmers to produce the food that we buy from shops and markets. Wild animals, however, have to find or catch their own food.

Humans use knives, forks, spoons or chopsticks to put food into their mouths. With food like this, it is cleaner than using your fingers.

Preparing food

Some of the foods we eat have to be washed, peeled or cooked before we eat them. Cooking kills **germs** and makes some food nicer to eat. Many foods, such as bread and biscuits, have already been cooked.

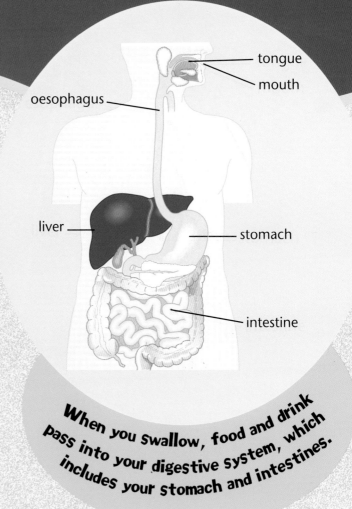

tongue
mouth
oesophagus
liver
stomach
intestine

When you swallow, food and drink pass into your digestive system, which includes your stomach and intestines.

Inside the body

What happens to food inside the body is similar in humans and animals. The food goes into your **stomach** and then into a long tube, called the **intestines**. The **nutrients** your body needs pass through the wall of the intestines into your blood. The rest is waste food, which leaves your body when you go to the toilet.

How animals eat

Animals usually eat and drink by putting their mouths into the food or water. Only a few animals, such as squirrels, apes and monkeys, hold food in their paws while they eat it.

Why I need to eat and drink

You eat because you feel hungry, but you don't eat just to fill your **stomach**. Food supplies your body with **energy** and with the **nutrients** it needs to grow and be healthy. Water is just as important as food, and you need to drink plenty of it to replace the water your body loses every day.

Energy for the body

You need energy for everything you do. You even use energy when you sleep. Your body uses food to get energy, like a car burns petrol to move.

Being active uses lots of energy. Your body gets energy from the food you eat.

Keeping healthy

Your body needs many different nutrients to work properly. It gets most of these from food. **Proteins** are needed to grow new **cells**. **Vitamins**, **minerals** and **fibre** keep your eyes, skin and all parts of your body working well.

How many meals?

Most people have three main meals a day, but animals, such as lions, often have one huge meal that lasts them for several days.

As this lion cub feeds on milk and meat, it will grow bigger and bigger, until it is the same size as its mother.

Food and energy

Some animals, such as cows and sheep, are herbivores. They eat only plants. Cats, dogs and many other animals are carnivores. They eat mainly meat.

Humans are omnivores because we can eat both plants and meat, although vegetarians choose not to eat meat. Whether you eat meat or not, you need to eat a wide range of food to get all the **nutrients** your body needs.

These foods all give your body energy because they contain starch, sugar or fat.

Nutrients

Most food contains a mixture of different nutrients. Cheese, for example, contains **protein** to help you grow, **vitamins** and minerals that make your skin and bones healthy, and fat that gives you **energy**.

Giraffes eat leaves, fruit and twigs. These plants give their bodies all the nutrients they need.

Energy food

Starch, sugar and fat are the nutrients that your body mainly uses to make energy. Rice and potatoes contain lots of starch and so do bread and pasta. Foods that contain sugar or fat also give you energy, but too much sugar or fat can be unhealthy.

Insect eaters

Some animals are insectivores. Hedgehogs, anteaters and bats, for example, get most of their protein from eating insects.

Food and health

Your body is made up of millions of tiny **cells**. Each cell needs **nutrients** so that it can keep working well.

Food that helps you grow

Meat, fish, nuts, beans and milk all contain **protein**. Your body uses protein to make new cells and to repair damaged cells. As you grow, your body makes millions of extra cells, so children need plenty of protein to grow well.

Measuring your height shows how much you have grown, but you cannot see the millions of cells that have been made to make you taller.

Fruit and vegetables

Most food contains some **vitamins** and **minerals**, but fruit and vegetables contain more of some important vitamins than other food. Fruit and vegetables also contain **fibre**. Fibre is important because it helps food to pass through your **intestines** more easily.

Looking at cells

Cells are too small to see with your eyes. We know what cells look like because we can see them through a **microscope**. This is what a bone cell looks like through a microscope. The microscope makes the cell look thousands of times bigger than it really is.

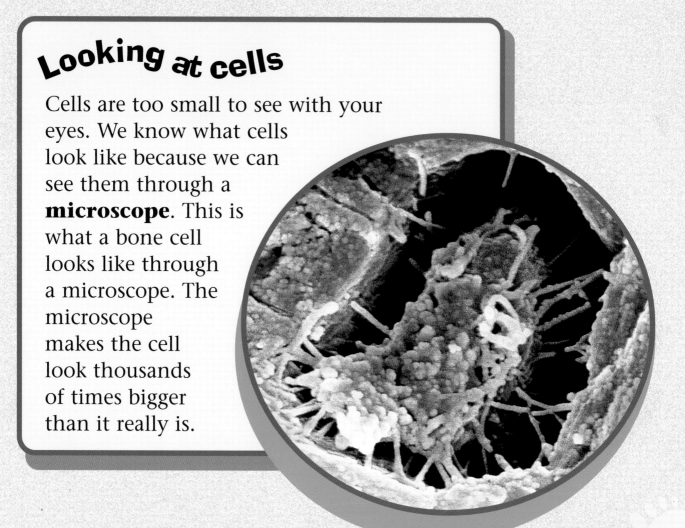

Drinking

Drinking water is the only way to quench your thirst. You probably enjoy drinking fruit juice, milk, soup and other liquids. All drinks are mainly water although some contain **nutrients**, too. All food contains some water, especially fruit and vegetables.

These girls are enjoying different drinks, but both drinks are made mainly of water.

Where the water goes

You need to drink to make up for the water that your body loses every day. You lose most water when you **urinate** and when you sweat. When you breathe out, the waste air also contains **water vapour**. Your body needs plenty of water because every **cell** contains it. Blood, saliva and other body **fluids** are also mainly water.

An elephant drinks by sucking water into its trunk and then squirting the water into its mouth.

Sipping and lapping

You probably drink from many kinds of containers, including cups and glasses. Wild animals drink straight from a pool or river. Many use their tongue to lap the water into their mouth.

Chewing

Before your body can use the **nutrients** in food, the food has to be broken down into tiny pieces. When you eat solid food, the first stage of breaking it down begins in your mouth.

Inside your mouth

You use your teeth and tongue to chew. Your front teeth bite into solid food, such as a carrot, and slice off a mouthful. Then you crush the carrot between the large teeth at the back of your mouth.

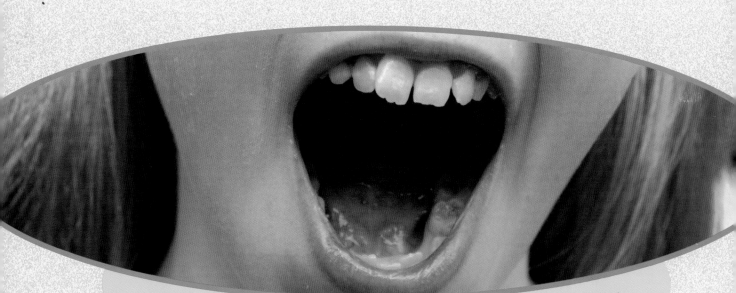

Your front teeth are sharp and flat for biting into hard food.

As you chew, your mouth makes extra liquid, called **saliva**. The pieces of food mix with the saliva and become mushy.

Birds' beaks

Birds have different shaped beaks, depending on the kind of food they eat. A duck has a flat beak for dabbling in water and an owl has a curved, sharp beak for tearing meat.

Animal teeth

The shape of an animal's teeth depends on the kind of food it mainly eats. Dogs have long, sharp fangs to grip on to and tear off meat. Sheep, and other animals that eat plants, have mainly flat teeth for grinding up grass and leaves.

The shape of a sheep's mouth and front teeth allows it to cut off blades of grass very close to the ground.

Swallowing

When the food in your mouth is well chewed up and mushy, your mouth gets it into a ball and your tongue pushes it to the back of your mouth. As soon as it hits the soft area at the back of your mouth, you cannot help but swallow it.

In your throat

Two tubes lead from your **throat**. One tube leads to your **stomach** and the other to your **lungs**. As you swallow, a flap called the **epiglottis** snaps shut across the tube to your lungs. Now the food can only go down the tube to your stomach.

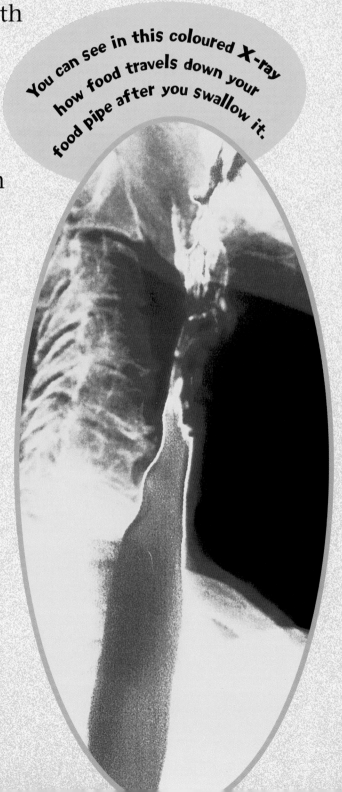

You can see in this coloured X-ray how food travels down your food pipe after you swallow it.

Down it goes

The tube that joins your mouth to your stomach is called the food pipe, or oesophagus. As the food slides down your food pipe, the walls of the tube tighten behind it. This squeezes the food down, like squeezing toothpaste from a tube.

Snake gobblers

Snakes swallow their food whole. Some snakes swallow animals that are wider than they are. The snake's body bulges as the huge meal moves slowly into its stomach.

Choking and vomiting

You choke or vomit when your body needs to get rid of something you have swallowed. Vomiting quickly empties your stomach. You choke when something gets stuck in your **throat**, or if food goes down the wrong way – into the tube that leads to your **lungs**.

When someone is choking, there is a special way of helping to dislodge the blockage. This is called the Heimlich maneuver, and only someone who has been properly trained can use it.

Choking

If you swallow a lump of food without chewing it first, it may stick in your throat and make you choke. Choking and coughing push food back into your mouth.

Vomiting

Vomiting gets rid of harmful **germs**. Usually the entrance to your stomach stays tightly closed after food has passed through it. When you vomit, however, your stomach forces the food back up your food pipe and out of your mouth.

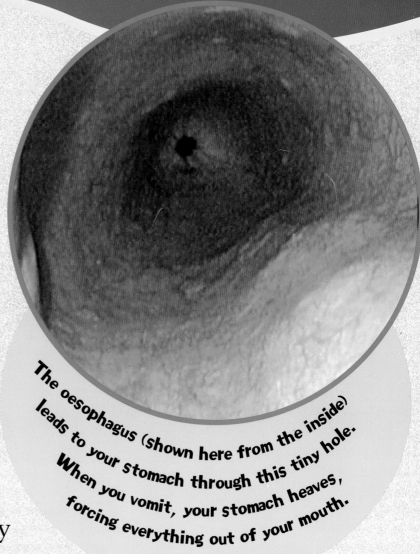

The oesophagus (shown here from the inside) leads to your stomach through this tiny hole. When you vomit, your stomach heaves, forcing everything out of your mouth.

Owl pellets

Owls swallow their **prey** whole and then vomit up pellets. These pellets contain feathers, bones, claws, beaks and any other bits of food their bodies do not want.

Digesting

Before your body can use food, it must be broken into tiny pieces. This process is called digestion, and chewing is only the start of it. The food you swallow goes down your food pipe into your **stomach**.

In your stomach

Your stomach is like a stretchy bag that squeezes and churns food. Food stays in your stomach for about 3 hours. Here, it mixes with juices made in your stomach and slowly changes into a kind of thick soup, called chyme.

As you can see in this X-ray, the coils of your intestine take up most of the space between your hips (bottom) and below your ribs (top).

In the intestines

Chyme squirts from your stomach into your **intestine**. More juices mix with the chyme, and break it into the different **nutrients**. The pieces are now so tiny the nutrients can pass through the wall of the intestine into your blood.

Chewing the cud

Grass is difficult to digest, even for cows, which have four stomachs to help them. After they have swallowed the grass, they bring it back up to chew again.

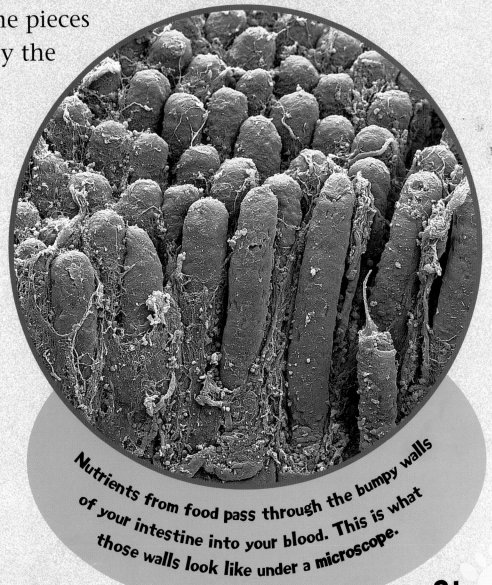

Nutrients from food pass through the bumpy walls of your intestine into your blood. This is what those walls look like under a microscope.

Getting rid of waste

Not all the food you eat passes into your blood. Some of it passes right through your **digestive system**. It is mixed with water and **bacteria** and is called faeces. Faeces leaves your body when you go to the toilet.

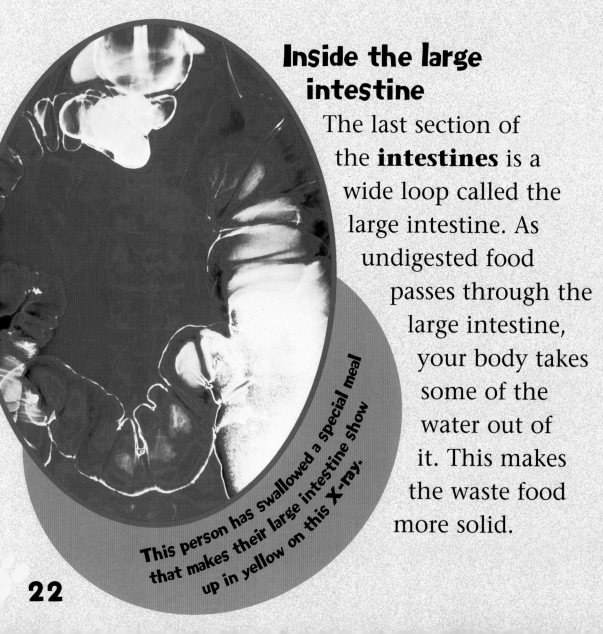

Inside the large intestine

The last section of the **intestines** is a wide loop called the large intestine. As undigested food passes through the large intestine, your body takes some of the water out of it. This makes the waste food more solid.

This person has swallowed a special meal that makes their large intestine show up in yellow on this **X-ray**.

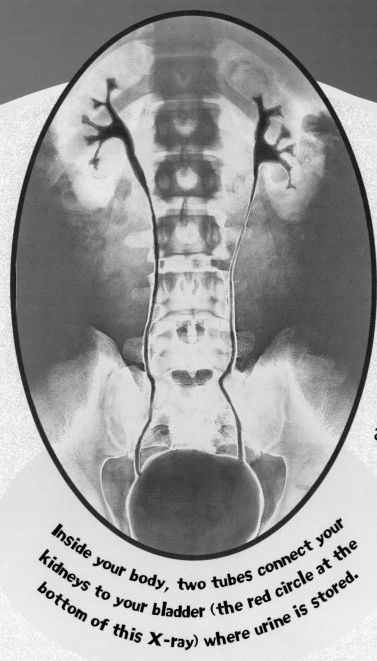

Inside your body, two tubes connect your kidneys to your bladder (the red circle at the bottom of this X-ray) where urine is stored.

Urine

Urine is extra water that your body does not need. Extra water is taken out of your blood in your **kidneys**. It is mixed with unwanted salt and a substance called urea. Urine trickles from your kidneys into your **bladder.** As your bladder fills up you feel the need to **urinate**.

Burping

You burp when you have too much gas in your **stomach.** Fizzy drinks contain gas that can make you burp, but your stomach produces extra gas too – particularly if you do not chew your food properly.

What can go wrong?

Things can go wrong in your **digestive system**. If you have a **stomach** ache after eating, it may be because you have swallowed some **germs**, or because there is too much gas in your stomach. Things can also go wrong with your teeth or your large intestine.

Tooth decay

If you eat lots of sweet, sugary food, the tough surface of your teeth gets worn away. If you get a hole in your tooth, it will give you toothache. It is important to clean your teeth every day and visit a dentist regularly.

Your dentist checks whether there are any holes in your teeth that need to be filled.

Stomach upsets

Sometimes germs get inside your stomach, perhaps from the food you eat. Germs can make you vomit or can cause stomach aches. It is important to always wash your hands before eating.

If you do not drink enough water or eat enough **fibre** you may suffer from constipation. The waste food in the large intestine gets too dry and hard for you to push it easily from your body.

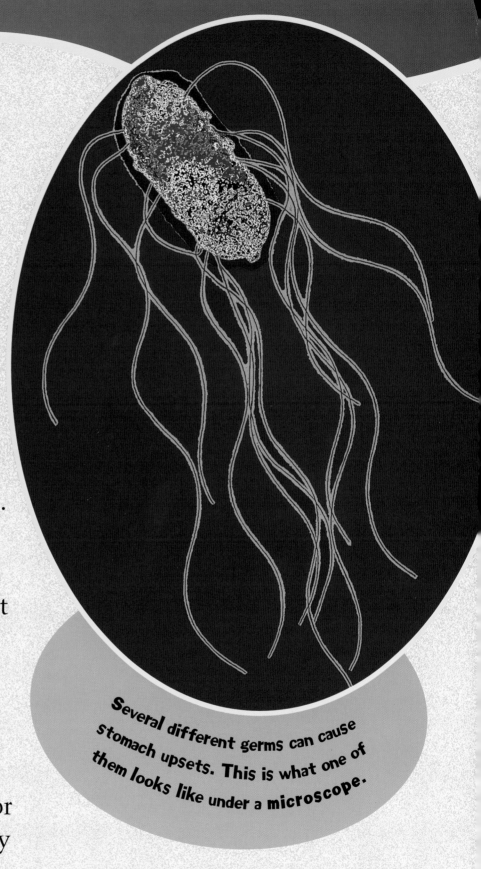

Several different germs can cause stomach upsets. This is what one of them looks like under a **microscope**.

Healthy eating

You need to eat many different foods to get all the **nutrients** that your body needs. You also need to eat more of some kinds of food than others.

Healthy food

About a third of the food you eat should be potatoes or cereals, such as bread, pasta and rice. This is the best food to give you **energy**. Another third of the food you eat should be fruit and vegetables. Meat, fish, cheese, milk and beans all help you to grow well. You should have two or three portions of this food every day.

These different foods contain some of the nutrients that your body needs to stay healthy.

Less healthy food

Sausages, cakes and many snacks contain a lot of sugar or fat. Too much of these foods can make you unhealthy. Too much sugar harms your teeth and too much fat can make you fat.

Pet food

Pets need to eat healthily too. A vet will know what kind of food your pet should eat. Cats or dogs should not eat sweet food, such as chocolate.

Raw fruit and vegetables are sweet but full of nutrients. They make good snacks if you feel hungry between meals.

The whole body

Eating and digesting food affects your whole body. The **nutrients** and water you swallow feed all of your **cells**. When you eat and drink, you also use more than just your **digestive system**.

Enjoying food

Your **senses** tell how food is likely to taste. If food looks and smells delicious, your mouth may begin to water. If food smells bad, you know not to eat it. Taste buds on your tongue taste the food.

You can use your sense of smell, to tell if food or drink has gone bad.

28

Feeding the cells

As food is digested, nutrients and water pass into your blood. Your **heart** pumps the blood to every cell in your body, including the cells in your brain and your skin. Each cell takes the **energy** and nutrients it needs from your blood. When your body needs more energy and other nutrients, you begin to feel hungry again.

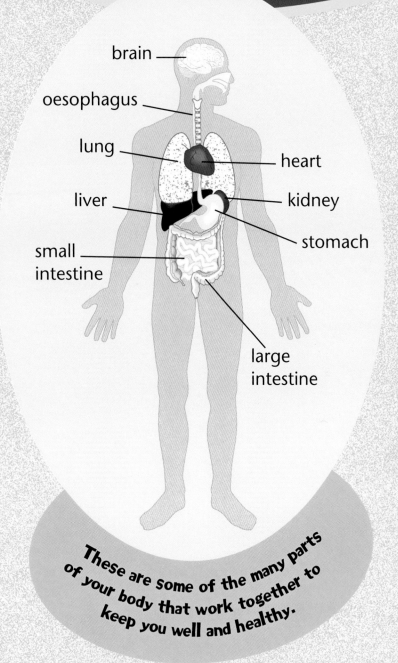

brain

oesophagus

lung

liver

small intestine

heart

kidney

stomach

large intestine

These are some of the many parts of your body that work together to keep you well and healthy.

Find out for yourself

Everybody's body is slightly different, but they all work in the same way. Find out more about how your own amazing body works by noticing what happens to it. What foods do you eat to supply your body with **protein**? How many times do you usually chew your food before you swallow it? What happens when you drink a lot of extra water? You will find the answers to many of your questions in this book, but you can also use other books and the Internet.

Books to read

Why do I vomit? And other questions about digestion, Angela Royston (Heinemann Library, 2002)

Look at your body: Digestion, S. Parker (Franklin Watts, 2001)

Body works: Eating, Paul Bennett (Belitha Press, 1998)

Using the Internet

Explore the Internet to find out more about food and eating. Websites can change, but if some of the links below no longer work, don't worry. Use a search engine, such as www.yahooligans.com or www.internet4kids.com, and type in keywords such as 'digestion', 'healthy food' or 'teeth'.

Websites:

www.kidshealth.org contains lots of information about how your body works and how to stay healthy

www.bbc.co.uk/science/humanbody/body contains an interactive body and lots of information. Click on stomach, small intestine and large intestine to find out more about eating and digesting.

www.innerbody.com contains information about the inside of your body.

Glossary

bacteria tiny living things that are made up of only one cell. Some kinds of bacteria can make you ill.

bladder stretchy bag inside your body that stores urine made in the kidneys

cell smallest building block of living things

digestive system parts of the body that work together to break up food into all the different nutrients

energy power to move or make something happen

epiglottis flap that covers the entrance to the windpipe when you swallow

fibre parts of plants that humans cannot digest

fluid usually a liquid, such as water

germ tiny form of life that can make you ill. Germs are so small you need a microscope to see them.

intestine long tube that carries waste from your stomach to the outside of your body

kidney part of the body that takes extra water, salt and waste from the blood to make urine. You have two kidneys.

lungs parts of the body that take in oxygen when you breathe in and get rid of waste carbon dioxide when you breathe out

microscope instrument that makes very tiny things look large enough to see

mineral chemical that is found in the ground and in some foods

nutrient chemicals in food that your body needs to get energy and stay healthy

prey animal that is caught and eaten by another animal

protein nutrient that your body needs to repair damaged cells and make new cells

saliva liquid made in the lining of your mouth

senses seeing, hearing, feeling, tasting and touching are your five senses

stomach part of the body where food goes after you have swallowed it

throat tube in the neck that joins the mouth to the oesophagus and windpipe

urinate let urine flow from your bladder out of your body

vitamin chemicals found in some foods that your body needs to stay healthy

water vapour water in the form of a gas

X-ray kind of photograph that shows parts of the inside of your body, such as your bones

Index

Raintree Perspectives version

Titles in the *My Amazing Body* series include:

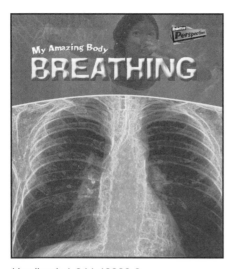

Hardback 1 844 43383 8

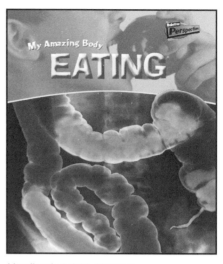

Hardback 1 844 43384 6

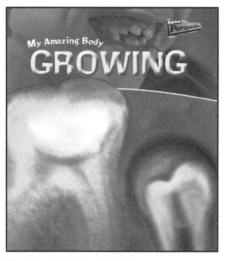

Hardback 1 844 43385 4

Hardback 1 844 43386 2

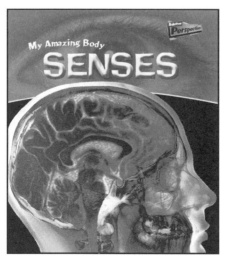

Hardback 1 844 43387 0

Hardback 1 844 43388 9

Find out about the other titles in this series on our website www.raintreepublishers.co.uk